A Grateful dispositi

All of us want to be happy, but how many of us make the effort to achieve it? One way to be happier is to be grateful. It may seem insignificant at first, but remember what life was like before gratitude became a habit.

Mindfulness has been shown to increase happiness, satisfaction and gratitude. People also report less stress when they are mindful as opposed to those who aren't mindful of their thoughts.

The power of gratitude is immense. When we take the time to appreciate what our lives have given us, like sleep or relationships with friends and family, we make them happier by being grateful. The practise of gratitude allows a person to appreciate these small pleasures throughout their daily routines, which brightens every aspect of their lives.

Gratitude makes every day an adventure worth living. No matter how bad the weather may be, being thankful will make your mood lighter and bring joy to those around you.

The key to living a happy life is to be grateful. You realize every day that nothing is as difficult as it seems, and your worries melt away. Additionally, when we are happy, everyday activities are less stressful. Who doesn't want more energy for fun things with friends or loved ones?

What are you most thankful for today?

_____

_____

_____

_____

_____

_____

_____

_____

_____

_____

_____

_____

_____

_____

_____

_____

Be thankful for small mercy's

Write down all the things you do on a daily basis,
but don't usually give much thought too.

For example; that could be a hot meal to eat, your eyesight, access to hot water.

_____

_____

_____

_____

_____

Write down who has made a difference
in your life.

Not just people that you know, but also total strangers. These people could have taught you something from a distance by their story or activities.
For example; a family member, best friend, significant other, an acquaintance, a person in the public eye or famous person.

_____

_____

_____

_____

_____

Write down times when you were most impressed with yourself.

For example; when you kept pursuing through a hard activity, when you were thoughtful towards a person, a job interview.

_____

_____

_____

_____

_____

_____

Write down the main five things that give you the feel-good factor.

For example; that could be watching a film, singing in the shower or your favourite meal.

_____

_____

_____

_____

_____

_____

Write down the most significant events in your life for which you are grateful.

For example; starting a family, overcoming an illness or escaping a near death experience.

_____

_____

_____

_____

_____

_____

_____

_____

_____

_____

_____

_____

_____

_____

_____

_____

_____

_____

_____

_____

_____

_____

_____

_____

_____

A penny for your thoughts.

An attitude of gratitude
brings great things.

When it comes to life, the most important
thing to consider is whether you
undervalue or value things.

Date ___/___/___.

I truly appreciate...

_____
_____
_____
_____
_____
_____
_____
_____

The nicest thing I noticed today......

_____
_____
_____
_____
_____
_____
_____
_____

A smile never hurt anyone! Let your personality shine by keeping a smile on the face of those around you.

Date ___/___/___.

I am fortunate for...

_____
_____
_____
_____
_____
_____
_____

Today has created my vision of tomorrow because......

_____
_____
_____
_____
_____
_____
_____

The secret to all abundance is gratitude, in order for you to attract more of what makes your life great, start by acknowledging the good things in it.

Date ___/___/___.

I truly appreciate...

_____
_____
_____
_____
_____
_____
_____

I kept my word today by doing......

_____
_____
_____
_____
_____
_____
_____

Expressing thanks goes a long way towards reminding people how much they mean to us, and gives them the opportunity to do something nice for someone else as well.

Date ___/___/___.

I am fortunate for...

_____
_____
_____
_____
_____
_____
_____

My life has given me an abundance of ...

_____
_____
_____
_____
_____
_____
_____

Cherish the relationships you have, as they are what makes life worth living.

Date ___/___/___.

I truly appreciate...

_____
_____
_____
_____
_____
_____
_____

Gratitude turned my routine job
I did today into a joy because ...

_____
_____
_____
_____
_____
_____
_____
_____

*Gratitude is fuel for the soul, it's what
makes us better people.*

Date ___/___/___.

I am fortunate for...

_____
_____
_____
_____
_____
_____
_____

I said thank you today approximately ...

_____
_____
_____
_____
_____
_____
_____

The heart has a memory that lasts forever. It's the way we remember those who have been important in our lives and how much they love us!

Date ___/___/___.

I truly appreciate...

_____
_____
_____
_____
_____
_____
_____

The kindest thing I did today was......

_____
_____
_____
_____
_____
_____
_____
_____
_____

When you are grateful for what's in front of you, the world looks like an endless garden.

Date ___/___/___.

I am fortunate for...

_____
_____
_____
_____
_____
_____
_____

Today I got to strengthen ....

_____
_____
_____
_____
_____
_____
_____

The power of small things can be immense.
It doesn't take much for something
big to happen.

Date ___/___/___.

I truly appreciate...

_____

_____

_____

_____

_____

_____

_____

Today taught me never to give up ......

_____

_____

_____

_____

_____

_____

_____

_____

Clear your mind and extend your life.

Date ___/___/___.

I am fortunate for...

_____
_____
_____
_____
_____
_____
_____

Today made me look on the bright side of life when......

_____
_____
_____
_____
_____
_____
_____
_____

Live in the moment, because you never know when you'll look back and realise these are some of your most treasured memories.

Date ___/___/___.

I truly appreciate...

_____
_____
_____
_____
_____
_____
_____

I am grateful I have come this far ....

_____
_____
_____
_____
_____
_____
_____
_____

One can never pay in gratitude, one must find a way to express thanks, either through words or actions.

Date ___/___/___.

I am fortunate for...

_____
_____
_____
_____
_____
_____
_____

A lot of time was saved for me when......

_____
_____
_____
_____
_____
_____
_____
_____
_____

When excellent things happen,
don't be surprised.

Date ___/____/____.

I truly appreciate...

_____
_____
_____
_____
_____
_____
_____
_____

I smiled when I received a message from.........

_____
_____
_____
_____
_____
_____
_____
_____
_____

You are a gift, your thoughtful actions deserve to be recognized and celebrated with kindness and trustworthiness, even love.

Date ___/___/___.

I am fortunate for...

_____
_____
_____
_____
_____
_____
_____

The one thing that a made a positive difference today was......

_____
_____
_____
_____
_____
_____
_____
_____

You are a valuable person, and your thoughtfulness is recognised and rewarded every day in many ways.

Date ___/____/____.

I truly appreciate...

_____
_____
_____
_____
_____
_____
_____

I felt over the moon today when
I was invited to......

_____
_____
_____
_____
_____
_____
_____

Happiness is a choice, not a result of circumstance.
Make your decision.

Date ___/____/____.

I am fortunate for...

_____
_____
_____
_____
_____
_____
_____

I felt proud when my opinion was
asked today......

_____
_____
_____
_____
_____
_____
_____

Gratitude is a powerful tool for developing one's character and sense of self worth.

Date ___/___/___.

I truly appreciate...

_____
_____
_____
_____
_____
_____
_____

My life today was enhanced when...

_____
_____
_____
_____
_____
_____
_____

The most valuable cash you'll ever
possess is gratitude.

Date ___/ ___/ ___.

I am fortunate for...

_____
_____
_____
_____
_____
_____
_____

The most thoughtful message
I received today was......

_____
_____
_____
_____
_____
_____
_____

You will be able to better take care of everyone in your life, when you are strong enough for yourself.

Date ___/___/___.

I truly appreciate...

_____
_____
_____
_____
_____

_____
_____
_____

The song that carried
me through the day was......

_____
_____
_____
_____
_____

_____
_____

You're not taking life too seriously,
if you can laugh at yourself.

Date ___/___/___.

I am fortunate for...

_____
_____
_____
_____
_____
_____
_____
_____

The first person to greet
me today was.........

_____
_____
_____
_____
_____
_____
_____
_____

*The greatest courage comes from within and
is discovered in self-dedication.*

Date ___/___/___.

I truly appreciate...

_____
_____
_____
_____
_____
_____
_____

Every day I am grateful that
I am able to.........

_____
_____
_____
_____
_____
_____
_____

First and foremost, love yourself.

Date ___/___/___ .

I am fortunate for...

_____
_____
_____
_____
_____
_____
_____

Today I did a random
act of kindness which was............

_____
_____
_____
_____
_____
_____
_____

Whatever life throws at you, you will always provide an opportunity for progress, so keep going.

Date ___/___/___.

I truly appreciate...

_____

_____

_____

_____

_____

_____

_____

My favourite phone call
I made today was.........

_____

_____

_____

_____

_____

_____

_____

Sometimes all you have to do is take a deep breath, trust your gut and wait to see what occurs.

Date ___/___/___.

I am fortunate for...

_____
_____
_____
_____
_____
_____
_____

The highlight of today
for me was............

_____
_____
_____
_____
_____
_____
_____

You are more than just another face in the crowd, you have a profound influence on others around you.

Date ___/___/___.

I truly appreciate...

_____
_____
_____
_____
_____
_____
_____

I did something today that
helped someone.........

_____
_____
_____
_____
_____
_____
_____

Getting up and trying again is sometimes
the bravest thing you can do.

Date ___/___/___ .

I am fortunate for...

_____
_____
_____
_____
_____
_____
_____

I felt over the moon today when
I was invited to......

_____
_____
_____
_____
_____
_____
_____

You are more than the sum of your circumstances; the "Upgrade" of you happens everyday.

Date ___/___/___.

I truly appreciate...

_____
_____
_____
_____
_____
_____
_____

This small thing I accomplished
today made me feel great because......

_____
_____
_____
_____
_____
_____
_____

The stories you tell yourself is the narrative to shape your life.

Date ___/___/___.

I am fortunate for...

_____
_____
_____
_____
_____
_____
_____

Today I had the simple pleasure of doing...........

_____
_____
_____
_____
_____
_____
_____

It's a lot simpler to get past other people's opinions about you, when you accept your worth, talents and strengths.

Date ___/____/____.

I truly appreciate...

_____
_____
_____
_____
_____
_____
_____

The most positive thing about
today was.........

_____
_____
_____
_____
_____
_____
_____

30 Day Reflection

My Thoughts

_____
_____
_____
_____
_____
_____

My Favourite Moments

_____
_____
_____
_____
_____
_____

What I Learned

_____
_____
_____
_____
_____
_____

It's fine to be imperfect; we all have defects, but that doesn't mean we can't strive to be better.

Date ___/___/___.

I truly appreciate...

_____

_____

_____

_____

_____

_____

_____

my favourite moment of the day was.........

_____

_____

_____

_____

_____

_____

_____

You have the ability to make a difference in someone's life every day.

Date ___/___/___.

I am fortunate for...

_____
_____
_____
_____
_____
_____
_____

I really value the time
I spent today ....

_____
_____
_____
_____
_____
_____
_____

It's not simple to be a winner in life, but if your thoughts and attitude reflect that, you are one. You have the ability to control your own destiny.

Date ___/___/___.

I truly appreciate...

_____
_____
_____
_____
_____
_____
_____

Today I was pleased to have spoken to.........

_____
_____
_____
_____
_____
_____
_____

You are more knowledgeable than you believe! You have a gut instinct for what is good and true.

Date ___/____/____.

I am fortunate for...

_____
_____
_____
_____
_____
_____
_____

Today I did spare a thought for ....

_____
_____
_____
_____
_____
_____
_____

Be your own masterpiece.

Date ___/___/___.

I truly appreciate...

_____

_____

_____

_____

_____

_____

_____

_____

Today I'm pleased to have learned.........

_____

_____

_____

_____

_____

_____

_____

How you're treated has nothing to do with who you are.

Date ___/___/___.

I am fortunate for...

_____
_____
_____
_____
_____
_____
_____

I was able to have some "me time" doing......

_____
_____
_____
_____
_____
_____
_____

Take little steps every day to ensure
steady growth.

Date ___/____/____.

I truly appreciate...

_____
_____
_____
_____
_____
_____
_____

Today I complimented myself for.........

_____
_____
_____
_____
_____
_____
_____

Self-assurance is a powerful force. When you believe in yourself, your dreams start to come true.

Date ___/___/___.

I am fortunate for...

_____

_____

_____

_____

_____

_____

_____

I smiled today when......

_____

_____

_____

_____

_____

_____

_____

Your energy is like a blazing neon light that attracts attention before you even get a chance to speak.

Date ___/___/___.

I truly appreciate...

_____
_____
_____
_____
_____
_____
_____

The meal I most enjoyed
today was.........

_____
_____
_____
_____
_____
_____
_____

There's always someone out in the world who would trade places with you anytime!!

Date ___/____/____.

I am fortunate for...

_____
_____
_____
_____
_____
_____
_____
_____

The time of the day I felt most relaxed was......

_____
_____
_____
_____
_____
_____
_____

A spirit of gratitude will keep
opportunities coming.

Date ___/____/____.

I truly appreciate...

_____

_____

_____

_____

_____

_____

_____

The good news I heard
today was.........

_____

_____

_____

_____

_____

_____

Returning gratitude is the most important task.

Date ___/___/___.

I am fortunate for...

_____
_____
_____
_____
_____
_____
_____

I had a good conversation today with......

_____
_____
_____
_____
_____
_____
_____

Make an effort to identify things to be grateful for and simply search for the good in yourself.

Date ___/___/___.

I truly appreciate...

_____

_____

_____

_____

_____

_____

_____

The wins I had today was.........

_____

_____

_____

_____

_____

_____

_____

A grateful heart is not only the greatest virtue but it also serves as the foundation for all other virtues.

Date ___/____/____.

I am fortunate for...

_____
_____
_____
_____
_____
_____
_____

Today has given me a deep appreciation for......

_____
_____
_____
_____
_____
_____
_____

What makes you grateful is not your bank balance, but the amount of love in your heart.

Date ___/____/____.

I truly appreciate...

_____
_____
_____
_____
_____
_____
_____

Today was interesting because.........

_____
_____
_____
_____
_____
_____
_____

A small thank you for a small favour is the key to getting bigger favours in return.

Date ___/___/___.

I am fortunate for...

_____
_____
_____
_____
_____
_____
_____

Today I got to work towards.........

_____
_____
_____
_____
_____
_____
_____

Gratitude is akin to electricity in that it must be produced, discharged and consumed in order to exist.

Date ___/___/____.

I truly appreciate...

_____
_____
_____
_____
_____
_____
_____

The nicest thing I heard today was.........

_____
_____
_____
_____
_____
_____
_____

Encouragement is more powerful
than correction.

Date ___/____/____.

I am fortunate for...

_____
_____
_____
_____
_____
_____
_____

I felt privileged today to be able to......

_____
_____
_____
_____
_____
_____

You won't be able to notice a shadow of you, if you keep your face to the light.

Date ___/___/____.

I truly appreciate...

_____
_____
_____
_____
_____
_____
_____

Today's feeling of being
able to do.........

_____
_____
_____
_____
_____
_____
_____

Small efforts, done day in and day out,
add up to success.

Date ___/___/___

I am fortunate for...

_____
_____
_____
_____
_____
_____
_____

The most thoughtful thing I saw today ......

_____
_____
_____
_____
_____
_____
_____

You've done it before and you'll be able to do it again.
Consider the favourable aspects.

Date ___/___/___.

I truly appreciate...

_____
_____
_____
_____
_____
_____
_____

Today my voice was actually heard when......

_____
_____
_____
_____
_____
_____
_____

What you do now has the potential to improve today and beyond.

Date ___/___/___.

I am fortunate for...

_____
_____
_____
_____
_____
_____
_____

Today made me realise I'm actually more satisfied with what I have in my life when......

_____
_____
_____
_____
_____
_____
_____

Begin where you are, make the most of what you
have and do your best.

Date ___/___/___.

I truly appreciate...

_____
_____
_____
_____
_____
_____
_____

My own life and experiences made me
so thankful today when......

_____
_____
_____
_____
_____
_____
_____

*You can achieve everything you set
your mind to.*

Date ___/___/___.

I am fortunate for...

_____
_____
_____
_____
_____
_____
_____

I was thought of first today when......

_____
_____
_____
_____
_____
_____

It appears impossible until its completed.

Date ___/___/___.

I truly appreciate...

_____

_____

_____

_____

_____

_____

_____

The feeling of being praised today when ......

_____

_____

_____

_____

_____

_____

_____

You are your most valuable asset, today is the day to invest in your most valuable asset.

Date ___/___/___.

I am fortunate for...

_____
_____
_____
_____
_____
_____
_____

I appreciated the patience that was shown
with me when ....

_____
_____
_____
_____
_____
_____
_____

Gratitude clarifies our past, brings serenity to the present and inspires a vision for the future.

Date ___/___/___.

I truly appreciate...

_____
_____
_____
_____
_____
_____
_____

The thoughtful gift I received today was ....

_____
_____
_____
_____
_____
_____
_____

The easiest method to make your dreams come true is to get out of bed in the morning.

Date ___/___/___.

I am fortunate for...

_____
_____
_____
_____
_____
_____
_____

Today's random act of
kindness was ......

_____
_____
_____
_____
_____
_____
_____

You can develop a mindset the same way
you develop a muscle.

Date ___/___/___.

I truly appreciate...

_____
_____
_____
_____
_____
_____
_____

My life was made easier today when ......

_____
_____
_____
_____
_____
_____
_____

30 Day Reflection

My Thoughts

_____
_____
_____
_____
_____
_____

My Favourite Moments

_____
_____
_____
_____
_____
_____

What I Learned

_____
_____
_____
_____
_____
_____

Have you ever gone looking for something just to discover that you already have it.

Date ___/___/___.

I am fortunate for...

_____
_____
_____
_____
_____
_____
_____

The little things that made the big difference today was......

_____
_____
_____
_____
_____
_____
_____

Be grateful for what you have right now, this is your life right now.

Date ___/___/___.

I truly appreciate...

_____
_____
_____
_____
_____
_____
_____
_____

Today my world was made a better place when......

_____
_____
_____
_____
_____
_____
_____

Gratitude and attitude are not challenges they are choices.

Date ___/___/___.

I am fortunate for...

_____
_____
_____
_____
_____
_____
_____

Today I was able to indulge in a passion that I had been too
busy to pursue on a regular basis, which was......

_____
_____
_____
_____
_____
_____
_____

What you do with what happens to you
is what matters.

Date ___/___/___.

I truly appreciate...

_____
_____
_____
_____
_____
_____
_____

Today I got to treat myself by......

_____
_____
_____
_____
_____
_____
_____

The best way to achieve success
is to earn it.

Date ___/___/___.

I am fortunate for...

_____
_____
_____
_____
_____
_____
_____

Today, I had the opportunity to live my greatest
life by doing......

_____
_____
_____
_____
_____
_____
_____

Do not be concerned about how the universe will reward you, it will.

Date ___/___/___.

I truly appreciate...

_____
_____
_____
_____
_____
_____
_____

Today, I had the opportunity to live my greatest life by doing......

_____
_____
_____
_____
_____
_____
_____

Give thanks in your own heart,
that will do it.

Date ___/___/___.

I am fortunate for...

_____

_____

_____

_____

_____

_____

_____

I can't complain today because I have so many
positive things in my life such as......

_____

_____

_____

_____

_____

_____

_____

Your imagination and commitment are the only limits to your effect.

Date ___/____/____.

I truly appreciate...

_____
_____
_____
_____
_____
_____
_____

Today was worth it because......

_____
_____
_____
_____
_____
_____
_____

Talk to yourself as if you were talking to someone you care about.

Date ___/___/___.

I am fortunate for...

_____
_____
_____
_____
_____
_____
_____

I chose to be appreciative today and this
happened for me......

_____
_____
_____
_____
_____
_____
_____

Although you can't control the wind,
you can change the sails.

Date ___/___/___.

I truly appreciate...

_____
_____
_____
_____
_____
_____
_____

Today was the first day I got to experience......

_____
_____
_____
_____
_____
_____
_____

Your most crucial relationship
is with yourself.

Date ___/___/___.

I am fortunate for...

_____
_____
_____
_____
_____
_____
_____

Today I got to learn from my mistake
by doing......

_____
_____
_____
_____
_____
_____
_____

If you disconnect it for a few minutes, almost everything, including you, will work again.

Date ___/____/____.

I truly appreciate...

_____
_____
_____
_____
_____
_____

The opportunity of the day I had was......

_____
_____
_____
_____
_____
_____
_____

Every voyage has hidden destinations that the traveller is unaware of.

Date ___/____/____.

I am fortunate for...

_____
_____
_____
_____
_____
_____
_____

I'm grateful for the information I received
today because......

_____
_____
_____
_____
_____
_____
_____

The journey is the teacher for the destination.

Date ___/___/___.

I truly appreciate...

_____

_____

_____

_____

_____

_____

My experience helped me out
today when......

_____

_____

_____

_____

_____

Your future will be what you plan.

Date ___/___/___.

I am fortunate for...

_____

_____

_____

_____

_____

_____

_____

Today I felt a sense of security......

_____

_____

_____

_____

_____

_____

_____

Don't chase happiness, you are happiness.

Date ___/___/___.

I truly appreciate...

_____

_____

_____

_____

_____

_____

_____

Today was valuable to me because......

_____

_____

_____

_____

_____

_____

_____

When you've experienced grace and know you've been forgiven, you're much more forgiving of others.

Date ___/___/___.

I am fortunate for...

_____
_____
_____
_____
_____
_____
_____

I made a difference today because......

_____
_____
_____
_____
_____
_____

A modest act of kindness does not exist.

Date ___/___/___.

I truly appreciate...

_____
_____
_____
_____
_____
_____
_____

Today I had the freedom to......

_____
_____
_____
_____
_____
_____

No one should be alone in the world and with kindness, we can help give them hope.

Date ___/___/___.

I am fortunate for...

_____
_____
_____
_____
_____
_____
_____

I expressed myself today by doing......

_____
_____
_____
_____
_____
_____
_____

Be thankful for the ones that
bring you joy.

Date ____ / ____ / ____ .

I truly appreciate...

_____
_____
_____
_____
_____
_____
_____

I expressed myself today
by doing......

_____
_____
_____
_____
_____
_____
_____

*Gratitude transforms what you
have into sufficient.*

Date ___/___/___.

I am fortunate for...

_____
_____
_____
_____
_____
_____
_____

Being able to see allowed me to view
the beauty......

_____
_____
_____
_____
_____
_____
_____

Being content does not imply that everything is ideal. It signifies you've decided to look past the flaws.

Date ___/___/___.

I truly appreciate...

_____
_____
_____
_____
_____
_____
_____

Today I got to enjoy the simple things
in life such as......

_____
_____
_____
_____
_____
_____

You were created to be authentic, not perfect.

Date ___/___/___.

I am fortunate for...

_____
_____
_____
_____
_____
_____
_____

Today I got to enjoy life by doing......

_____
_____
_____
_____
_____
_____
_____

The mind is capable of doing whatever
it can imagine and believe.

Date ___/____/____.

I am truly appreciative...

_____

_____

_____

_____

_____

_____

_____

My life was made easier today
by being able to......

_____

_____

_____

_____

_____

_____

_____

Where you water the grass,
it grows greener.

Date ___/____/____.

I am fortunate for...

_____
_____
_____
_____
_____
_____
_____

Today I found comfort in......

_____
_____
_____
_____
_____
_____
_____

Smile because it happened.

Date ___/____/____.

I am truly appreciative...

_____
_____
_____
_____
_____
_____
_____

I felt good within myself because......

_____
_____
_____
_____
_____
_____
_____

Aspire to inspire.

Date ___/___/___.

I am fortunate for...

_____
_____
_____
_____
_____
_____
_____

It felt good today when I heard
the voice of......

_____
_____
_____
_____
_____
_____

It's not about getting knocked down,
it's about getting up.

Date ___/____/____.

I am truly appreciative...

_____
_____
_____
_____
_____
_____
_____

My outlook on outcomes came in handy
today when......

_____
_____
_____
_____
_____
_____
_____

*Opportunity can be found in the
midst of adversity.*

Date ___/____/____.

I am fortunate for...

_____
_____
_____
_____
_____
_____
_____

I had the time today to......

_____
_____
_____
_____
_____
_____
_____

30 Day Reflection

My highlights

_____
_____
_____
_____
_____
_____

A few things I discovered

_____
_____
_____
_____
_____
_____

My opinion

_____
_____
_____
_____
_____
_____

VISIONING THE FUTURE

WHAT I PLAN ON DOING

_____
_____
_____
_____
_____

IMPROVEMENTS TO BE MADE

_____
_____
_____
_____
_____
_____

THE FUTURE IS LOOKING
BRIGHT BECAUSE

_____
_____
_____
_____
_____
_____

I feel so grateful

Tick the box below

Go ahead and express whatever is on your mind.

_____

_____

_____

_____

_____

_____

_____

_____

_____

_____

_____

_____

_____

_____

_____

_____

_____

_____

_____

_____

_____

A BIG THANK YOU

This journal has been designed to help you take care of yourself. It was created with the mindfulness that we all need so time just for ourselves and our mission is to create better lives through books one page at a time!

We are always looking at ways to improve our journals and would love any feedback on how we can make them better! If there's something in particular that you would like to see included, please don't hesitate to get in touch with us at

thisissohelpful471@gmail.com

We appreciate each and every one of you please
leave an honest review.